from SEA TO SHINING SEA
WISCONSIN

By Dennis Brindell Fradin

CONSULTANTS

Howard Kanetzke, Curator of Education, State Historical Museum, Madison

Robert L. Hillerich, Ph.D., Consultant, Pinellas County Schools, Florida;
Visiting Professor, University of South Florida

CHILDRENS PRESS®
CHICAGO

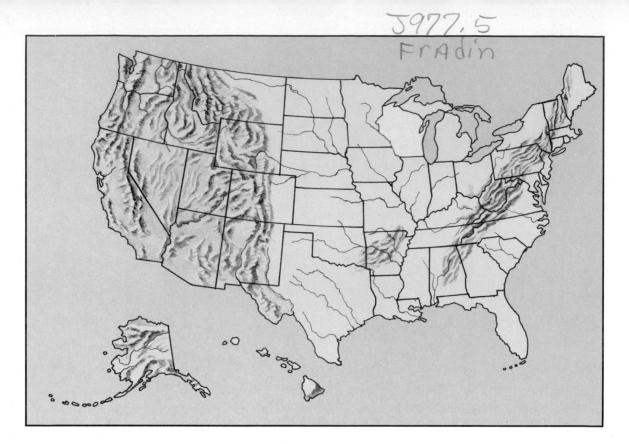

Wisconsin is one of the twelve states in the region called the Midwest. The other Midwest states are Illinois, Michigan, Indiana, Iowa, Ohio, Minnesota, Missouri, Nebraska, North Dakota, South Dakota, and Kansas.

For my wonderful brother-in-law, David Polster, with love

Front cover picture: A dairy farm near Mount Calvary; page 1: trees on a ridge, Richland Center; back cover: Cave Point County Park, Door County

Project Editor: Joan Downing
Design Director: Karen Kohn
Research Assistant: Judith Bloom Fradin
Typesetting: Graphic Connections, Inc.
Engraving: Liberty Photoengraving

Library of Congress Cataloging-in-Publication Data

Fradin, Dennis B.
  Wisconsin / by Dennis Brindell Fradin.
   p.   cm. — (From sea to shining sea)
  Includes index.
  Summary: An overview of the Badger State, introducing
its history, geography, industries, sites of interest, and
famous people.
  ISBN 0-516-03849-4
  1. Wisconsin—Juvenile literature. [1. Wisconsin.]
I. Title. II. Series: Fradin, Dennis B.
From sea to shining sea.
F581.3.F72   1992   92-8135
977.5—dc20   CIP
                                                 AC

A young Wisconsin boy with his horses

Table of Contents

INTRODUCING THE BADGER STATE

Wisconsin is in the midwestern United States. It is the top milk-producing state. Wisconsin also leads the country at making such milk products as butter and cheese. Because of these things, Wisconsin is called "America's Dairyland." Its main nickname, however, is the "Badger State." Long ago, Wisconsin miners lived in caves dug in hills. This reminded people of how badgers live.

A badger is an animal that digs a hole in the ground to live in.

Wisconsin's motto is "Forward." Over the years, Wisconsin has led the country forward in many ways. Margarethe Schurz opened the country's first kindergarten in Wisconsin. The anti-slavery Republican party began there. The typewriter was invented in Milwaukee.

Wisconsin has made its mark on the country in many other ways. What state was first to pass a law to provide money for jobless people? Where was malted milk invented? Where were children's authors Laura Ingalls Wilder and Marguerite Henry born? Where do the Green Bay Packers and the Milwaukee Brewers play? The answer to all these questions is: Wisconsin, the Badger State!

A picture map
of Wisconsin

A Land of Lakes
and Woods

A Land of Lakes and Woods

Wisconsin is one of twelve states that make up the region called the Midwest. Four other midwestern states border Wisconsin. Illinois is to the south. Iowa and Minnesota are to the west. Upper Michigan is to the north.

Wisconsin is a Great Lakes state. Two of the five Great Lakes border Wisconsin. Lake Superior forms part of the state's northern border. Lake Michigan bathes Wisconsin's entire eastern shore. Wisconsin owns several islands in both lakes.

Geography

Wisconsin is sometimes called "The Land of Lakes." There are about fifteen thousand lakes in the state. The largest is Lake Winnebago. It takes up 215 square miles.

Many rivers run through the Badger State. The Mississippi and St. Croix rivers separate Wisconsin from its western neighbors. Other Wisconsin rivers include the Wisconsin, the Chippewa, the Rock, the Wolf, the Fox, and the Black.

Pages 6-7: Grandfather Falls on the Wisconsin River, Ice Age National Scenic Trail

Lake Superior (below) is the world's largest freshwater lake.

8

Hundreds of waterfalls are formed where the rivers flow over cliffs. Big Manitou Falls is on the Black River. It drops 165 feet and is the state's highest waterfall.

The Badger State has long stretches of flat land. Parts of northern and western Wisconsin are hilly. There are no large mountains in the state, however. Wisconsin's highest point is Timms Hill. It is only 1,952 feet above sea level. The western United States has peaks about ten times that high.

About half of Wisconsin is covered with forest. The state's most-wooded region is its northern third. This area is often called the "North Woods."

The St. Croix River (left) forms part of the border between Wisconsin and Minnesota.

9

Left: Birch trees in Chequamegon National Forest
Right: Ferns in a narrow canyon at the Wisconsin Dells

In places, hikers can walk for hours and see nothing but trees and lakes. Some of Wisconsin's trees are ash, maple, yellow birch, pine, and tamarack.

CLIMATE

Because Wisconsin is a northern state, it has cold winters. Winter temperatures in northern Wisconsin often fall below minus 30 degrees Fahrenheit. The temperature in Danbury fell to minus 54 degrees Fahrenheit on January 24, 1922. This was the low-

est temperature ever recorded in the state. Only eight states have ever recorded a colder temperature. Wisconsin also has heavy snowfalls. Each year, northern Wisconsin receives about 100 inches of snow. That is why cross-country skiing and snow-mobiling are popular there.

Wisconsin's summers are warm, however. On some summer days, temperatures rise to over 90 degrees Fahrenheit. The state's highest temperature was 114 degrees Fahrenheit. That record was set on July 13, 1936, at the Wisconsin Dells.

Wisconsin's cold and snowy winters are good for cross-country skiing (left) and for forming beautiful ice falls (right).

Overleaf: Women working in the vegetable garden in the Finnish area of Old World Wisconsin, near Eagle

From Ancient Times Until Today

FROM ANCIENT TIMES UNTIL TODAY

About two million years ago, the Ice Age began. Masses of ice called glaciers covered most of Wisconsin. As the glaciers moved, they ground down hilltops. This left much of Wisconsin smooth and flat. All the glaciers went around southwest Wisconsin. So that part of the state has rugged hills.

The glaciers also scooped out some giant holes. These holes filled with water and became the Great Lakes. The many lakes inside Wisconsin were formed by melted ice left behind by the glaciers.

AMERICAN INDIANS

People first reached Wisconsin about twelve thousand years ago. The Ice Age was ending at about that time. The first Wisconsinites were hunters who followed herds of mammoths and other large animals.

By about A.D. 500, Indians with different ways of life were living in the area. They are known for the huge dirt mounds they built. Some mounds were shaped like giant animals. Lizard Mound Park

Mammoths no longer exist. They were huge, hairy animals that looked much like today's elephants.

is near West Bend. It has mounds that look like a lizard, a bird, and a wildcat.

Later, many American Indian tribes lived in Wisconsin. They included the Menominee, Winnebago, Sauk, Fox, Miami, and Chippewa. The Chippewa moved from place to place. They hunted and fished for food. They built canoes and paddled them across Wisconsin's lakes and along its rivers. Many groups lived in villages in the summertime. They grew corn, squash, and beans. They also hunted deer in the woods and fished in the streams. In winter, family groups followed the game to sheltered valleys.

The word *Wisconsin* comes from *Weeskonsan.* That was the Chippewa name for the Wisconsin River. It is thought to mean "the gathering of waters."

Wisconsin's woodland Indians farmed, fished, and hunted during the summers.

FRENCH EXPLORERS AND FUR TRADERS

In the early 1600s, people from France started settling in Canada. They called this land New France. French fur traders in Canada soon grew interested in the land to the south. They hoped to find more furs and meet more American Indians. They also hoped to find a water route to China. China, they

China is really about 8,000 miles west of Wisconsin, across the Pacific Ocean.

knew, had many treasures, including spices to preserve food.

French explorer Jean Nicolet set out from Canada in 1634. He canoed across Lake Michigan. That fall, he landed north of the present-day city of Green Bay. Nicolet thought he might be in China. Before leaving his canoe, Nicolet dressed in a fancy robe. But Chinese leaders did not greet Nicolet. Instead, he was met by Winnebago Indians.

During the 1650s, two French fur traders explored Wisconsin. They were Pierre Esprit, Sieur de Radisson, and his brother-in-law, Medard

Left: This guide at Heritage Hills State Park in Green Bay is dressed as a French fur trader.
Right: A statue of explorer Jean Nicolet

Chouart, Sieur des Groseilliers. In the 1660s, French priests went to Wisconsin. They built missions. These were small settlements based around a church. In 1672, the French claimed Wisconsin. In 1673, Father Jacques Marquette and Louis Jolliet explored Wisconsin.

During these years, more French fur traders arrived. Some of them stayed in Wisconsin and built trading posts. Some brought their families from Canada. Some married Indian women. Important French settlements were built at Green Bay and Prairie du Chien.

ENGLAND RULES WISCONSIN

While the French explored New France, England settled thirteen colonies. They were along the Atlantic Ocean. The English also traded for furs with the Indians.

From 1754 to 1763, France and England fought a war. It decided which country would control North America. No major fighting took place in Wisconsin. Yet, England's victory was important to the region. The English got France's land in Canada. They also got most of France's land east of the Mississippi River. This included Wisconsin.

Some guides at Heritage Hills are costumed as British soldiers.

These miners' homes at Mineral Point have been restored.

The Americans Take Over

A territory is land owned by a country.

In 1775, the thirteen colonies in the eastern part of America rebelled against English rule. This was the start of the Revolutionary War. The Americans finally won their independence from England in 1783. Wisconsin then became part of the new nation—the United States of America. Wisconsin didn't become a state right away. Instead, it was a territory of the United States for many years.

Wisconsin grew quickly under the American flag. Southwest Wisconsin proved to be rich in lead ore. Miners were the first to move there. Many of

18

them lived for a time in caves dug into hillsides. But most of them soon built homes and towns. Later, farm families moved there. They built log cabins and grew corn and wheat.

Dodgeville, Platteville, and Mineral Point were important lead-mining towns. They were founded in southwest Wisconsin before 1830. Towns were also growing in other parts of Wisconsin. Present-day Milwaukee and Oshkosh were settled in 1818. Racine, Kenosha, Madison, and Sheboygan were all settled during the 1830s.

By the 1830s, southwest Wisconsin was the nation's top lead-mining region.

During those years, the American Indians were losing their lands to the newcomers. Most of the Sauk and Fox Indians had moved to Iowa, west of the Mississippi River. In 1832, Sauk chief Black Hawk led Sauk and Fox Indians back from Iowa. They fought settlers and soldiers in Illinois and Wisconsin.

The Black Hawk War didn't last long. On August 1-2, 1832, the Indians suffered a crushing defeat. This happened at the Battle of Bad Axe in southwest Wisconsin. The Indians tried to recross the Mississippi River. But they were attacked by United States troops. About five hundred Indians were killed. After this battle, the Indians lacked the strength to fight the settlers.

Sauk chief Black Hawk

STATEHOOD

After the Black Hawk War, more people came to Wisconsin. They came from Illinois and Missouri and from the New England states. They also came from Germany, England, Ireland, Norway, and Switzerland. By the late 1840s, Wisconsin had more than 200,000 people. This was more than enough for statehood. The United States Congress made Wisconsin the thirtieth state on May 29, 1848. Madison was the state capital, as it still is.

Wisconsin's early settlers valued education. They founded good schools. The University of Wisconsin opened in 1849 in Madison. In 1856, Margarethe Schurz founded the first kindergarten in the United States. It opened in Watertown. The Wisconsin constitution (1848) provided for free schools.

The capitol in Madison, 1851

THE CIVIL WAR

When Wisconsin became a state, Americans were arguing over slavery. The southern states allowed people to own black slaves. Slavery had been outlawed in Wisconsin and in the other northern states.

Some antislavery people met at Ripon in 1854.

They began a new political party. One of its main goals was fighting slavery. They called themselves Republicans. They joined other people with similar views who met in other places. The Republicans grew into one of the country's two big political parties.

The arguing over slavery finally led to the Civil War (1861-1865). On one side were the Confederate (southern) states. Against them were the Union (northern) states. About 90,000 Wisconsin men fought for the North.

By the time the North won the war, about 12,000 Wisconsin men had died. One good thing came out of the Civil War. All the slaves were freed.

The Milton House was once a stagecoach inn that served as a stop on the Underground Railroad. Slaves escaping to Canada hid there in an underground tunnel.

There were no Civil War battles in Wisconsin. But Wisconsin troops fought in many places during the war.

LUMBER, DAIRIES, AND MANUFACTURING

After the Civil War, lumber companies sent lumber-jacks into the Wisconsin woods. These strong men cut down millions of trees. From 1870 until the early 1900s, Wisconsin was a leading lumber state.

The lumberjacks tried to outdo each other telling tall tales. Many stories were told about a giant lumberjack named Paul Bunyan. Glaciers created Wisconsin's lakes. But the lumberjacks said that Paul Bunyan's huge footprints had dug them out.

The lumber companies cut whole forests down. They did not plant new trees. By the late 1800s, the

Left: Lumberjacks working in the woods of Wisconsin
Right: The Peshtigo Fire of 1871

trees were gone from much of northern Wisconsin. Forest fires added to the damage.

The deadliest fire in United States history struck Wisconsin in 1871. That summer was hot and dry. By early fall, many forest fires were burning. A huge fire raced toward Peshtigo on October 8, 1871. The fire destroyed that town. It killed about twelve hundred people in and around the town.

Wisconsin's dairy industry was growing during this same time. Much of the state's land had become worn-out from planting crops such as wheat. Many farmers started raising dairy cows and selling milk.

William Dempster Hoard and Dr. Stephen Babcock helped make Wisconsin a great dairy state. Hoard helped found the Wisconsin Dairymen's Association in 1872. It worked to improve dairy farming in the state. Hoard became known as "The Father of Modern Dairying." Babcock taught at the University of Wisconsin, in Madison. He developed the Babcock Test in 1890. The test measured the amount of butterfat in milk. The quality of Wisconsin butter improved because of this test.

Hoard was Wisconsin's governor from 1889 to 1891.

Manufacturing was also growing. Wisconsin lumber was made into a variety of goods. By the 1880s, Oshkosh led the country at making wooden

Before there were refrigerators, people kept food cold in iceboxes.

doors and wagons. Workers in Kenosha made wooden beds. Those in Sheboygan made chairs. Fond du Lac workers produced wooden iceboxes.

Food packaging also became important. Milwaukee's breweries made much of the Midwest's beer. Madison and Milwaukee became meat-packing centers. Cheese was made in many places.

Life was very hard for the factory workers of the late 1800s. Fourteen-hour days were common. Pay was low. Conditions were dangerous. Robert M. La Follette was Wisconsin's governor from 1901 to 1906. He was a United States senator from 1906 to 1925. "Fighting Bob" worked to improve Wisconsin in many ways.

In 1911, Wisconsin passed laws to help workers. Factories were made safer. Workdays were shortened for children and women. Factory owners had to pay the families of workers who were injured or killed. Wisconsin was one of the first states to make such laws.

WARS, DEPRESSION, AND MCCARTHYISM

In 1917, the United States entered World War I (1914-1918). About 120,000 Wisconsin men and women served during the war. Other Wisconsinites

Robert M. "Fighting Bob" La Follette

worked in factories that made goods for the war. They all helped the United States and its allies win.

A few years later, the Great Depression struck the United States. The hard times lasted from 1929 to 1939. Factories closed in Milwaukee and other cities. This cost thousands of Wisconsinites their jobs. Many families lost their farms. Governor Philip La Follette helped Wisconsin survive the Great Depression. He was "Fighting Bob's" son. In 1932, Wisconsin passed a law to provide money for jobless people. It was the first state to do this.

Philip La Follette was Wisconsin's governor from 1931 to 1933 and from 1935 to 1939.

World War II (1939-1945) helped bring an end to the Great Depression. The United States entered the war in 1941. About 300,000 Wisconsin men and women took part in the war. Major Richard Bong shot down forty enemy planes—more than any other United States pilot. Milwaukee mayor Carl Zeidler left office to join the navy. Zeidler's

Major Richard Bong (left) was from Poplar, near Lake Superior, in northwest Wisconsin.

Senator Joseph McCarthy points to a map during the Army-McCarthy hearings.

Communism is a system in which the government owns most of the property.

ship sank. He was one of 8,000 Wisconsinites who died helping win World War II.

A sad chapter in American history occurred during the 1950s. A fear of communism swept the nation. At that time, the Soviet Union was ruled by Communists. Its people weren't allowed to take part in government. The Soviet Union had taken over many Eastern European countries. Those governments were forced to accept communism.

Some Americans feared that Communists would also take over the United States. They began saying that some Americans were Communists. Wisconsin senator Joseph McCarthy led the United States attacks against so-called American Communists. He accused people in the United States Army and the government of being Communists. McCarthy helped create a climate of fear. Many innocent people were accused of being Communists. They lost their jobs.

Americans finally saw that this name-calling was wrong. The Communist scare died down around the time of McCarthy's death in 1957. His name became part of a new word—McCarthyism. When government officials pick on others unfairly, they are said to be guilty of McCarthyism.

THE MODERN STATE AND ITS PROBLEMS

In the 1960s, the United States became involved in the Vietnam War (1964-1973). This was a war in Southeast Asia. Many Americans opposed this war. The University of Wisconsin at Madison became a center of war protest. In May 1972, 10,000 war protesters gathered at the university. They held a candlelight march on May 9. Finally, in 1973, the nation pulled out of the war. About 1,250 Wisconsinites had died in the fighting.

Meanwhile, Wisconsin was changing. Manufacturing grew. Many farmers had moved to cities to work in factories. In 1930, more Wisconsinites lived in cities than in small towns. By 1990, twice as many Wisconsinites lived in cities as in small towns.

In 1972, Vietnam War protesters gathered at the University of Wisconsin (above).

Children who live on farms do chores such as collecting eggs.

Reservations are lands that have been set aside for American Indians.

Many people didn't leave their farms by choice. The cost of seed, feed, and farm equipment went up. But prices paid to farmers for milk and other farm goods were low. This forced thousands of farmers to give up their land. As recently as 1980, there were about 93,000 farms in Wisconsin. By 1991, there were only about 79,000.

The growth of Wisconsin's cities also created problems. Factories, cars, and people caused pollution. By 1990, the air in Milwaukee was at times unhealthy to breathe. This was also true of other Wisconsin cities. Factories and plants dumped harmful chemicals into Lakes Michigan and Superior. The Fox River is also polluted.

Milwaukee has huge problems. The city beautified its downtown during the 1980s. However, many Milwaukee neighborhoods need help. High crime rates trouble those neighborhoods. Young people in those areas drop out of school at a high rate. Blacks in the city have suffered the most. By 1990, one in every six black Milwaukeeans was out of work. This was six times the jobless rate of white Milwaukeeans.

Wisconsin's American Indians have also suffered. Half the adults on some reservations cannot find work. The Chippewas have had an added problem.

They have certain fishing rights that other people don't have. During the 1980s, some whites claimed that the Chippewas caught too many fish. They said that this kept some tourists from going to northern Wisconsin to fish. White people threatened Chippewas as they fished. Some even threw rocks at them.

Wisconsinites are trying to solve their problems. A study released in 1991 showed that Chippewa fishing did not endanger the fish supply. By 1992, the fight over Chippewa fishing rights was calming down. Tommy Thompson was elected governor in 1986. He began many new programs. Some of those programs dealt with poverty in Wisconsin. Wisconsin has also begun some outstanding programs to fight pollution.

Even though Milwaukee has some problems, the city prides itself in its friendly people and its cleanliness.

Wisconsinites and Their Work

WISCONSINITES AND THEIR WORK

As a group, Wisconsinites are among the best-educated Americans. Most of them also love the outdoors. Boating and fishing are favorite pastimes in the Badger State. Snowmobiling and cross-country skiing are popular winter sports. The United States Census counted 4,891,769 Wisconsinites in 1990. Only fifteen states had more people.

A little more than half of all Wisconsinites have some German ancestry. No other state has as high a percentage of German Americans. The state also has many people of Norwegian, Danish, Swedish, and Finnish backgrounds. Others have English, Irish, Scottish, Swiss, and Polish backgrounds. About

Opposite: A father carries his child in a bushel basket on the family farm at pumpkin harvest time.

Many Wisconsinites are of Polish (left) or German (right) ancestry.

Only thirteen states have more American Indians than Wisconsin.

250,000 Wisconsinites are black. Another 100,000 are Hispanic. About 40,000 American Indians make their homes in the state. More than 21,000 American Indians live on Wisconsin's eleven Indian reservations. Others live in towns and cities around the state.

How They Earn Their Living

Manufacturing brings in more money than any other kind of work in Wisconsin. More than 500,000 Wisconsinites work in factories. They make Wisconsin one of the top fifteen manufacturing states.

Machinery, paper goods, and foods are the state's leading products. Wisconsin is America's top maker of farm machines. They range from tractors to milking machines. Wisconsin leads the nation at making paper. It also packages more milk, butter, and cheese than any other state. Other products include meat, beer, ice cream, auto engines and parts, and furniture.

Another 500,000 Wisconsinites sell goods. About 350,000 work for the government. Wisconsin is a popular vacationland. Therefore, tourism provides jobs for thousands of other people.

Two of Wisconsin's important products are cheese (left) and produce (right).

They work at historic attractions, restaurants, resorts, and hotels.

About 80,000 Wisconsin families live on farms. Milk is Wisconsin's number-one farm product. Each year, the state produces three billion gallons of milk. That is more milk than any other state produces. This could provide every American with a quart of milk each week.

Wisconsin also leads the nation at growing snap beans, peas, and beets. Wisconsin's farmers also grow sweet corn, barley, and hay. Wisconsin is among the top five growers of cranberries, carrots, and cucumbers for pickles. In addition, Wisconsin's farmers raise large numbers of hogs and beef cattle.

Overleaf: Fish Creek Lighthouse, Door County

A Trip
Through
Wisconsin

A Trip Through Wisconsin

Wisconsin is a great state to visit. It has beautiful lakes and woods. It has interesting cities. Along its roadsides, stores offer such treats as ice cream and cheese.

Southeast Wisconsin

Wisconsin's southeastern corner has the most people. Kenosha, Racine, and Milwaukee are in this area. They lie along Lake Michigan. They are three of the state's five largest cities.

Families from New York State began Kenosha in 1835. Newspaper editor Christopher Sholes was an early Kenosha settler. In 1867, Sholes helped invent the typewriter. Today, Kenosha is Wisconsin's fifth-biggest city.

Racine is north of Kenosha. It was also settled during the 1830s. One of the first automobiles was built there in 1873. It was built by Dr. John W. Carhart. He was a Racine physician and a minister. Dr. Carhart drove around Racine at about 5 miles per hour in his steam-powered buggy! In 1887, William Horlick invented malted milk in Racine.

Below: A Sholes typewriter

Today, Racine is Wisconsin's fourth-largest city. The Johnson Wax Company's headquarters is in Racine. The building was designed by famed Wisconsin architect Frank Lloyd Wright.

Milwaukee is north of Racine. Fur trader Solomon Juneau first arrived in 1818. He began Juneautown in 1833. Within a few years, the name was changed to Milwaukee.

Milwaukee's fine location on Lake Michigan helped it grow. Today, Milwaukee is the state's largest city by far.

Milwaukee has long been a beer-brewing center. Visitors can tour a brewery to see how beer is made. They can also tour the thirty-seven-room Pabst Mansion. It was built by brewer Frederick Pabst in

Above: Milwaukee Community Sailing Club

Architects decide what a building will look like and how it will be built.

1893. Two years later, Pabst built Milwaukee's Pabst Theater. Concerts, plays, and children's shows are performed in this carefully restored theater.

Many people visit Milwaukee just to see the Milwaukee County Zoo. This was one of America's first zoos in which the animals were not caged. They roam freely in natural settings. Mitchell Park Conservatory is another highlight of Milwaukee. Rare plants in three huge, glass-domed greenhouses can be seen there. Visitors to the Milwaukee Public Museum can walk the "Streets of Old Milwaukee." That exhibit shows how the city looked a hundred years ago. Milwaukee is also home to the Brewers of major-league baseball and the Bucks of pro basketball.

Because Milwaukee has many people of German background, the city celebrates *Oktoberfest*. That is a

The Milwaukee Brewers won the American League pennant in 1982. The Milwaukee Bucks won the pro basketball championship in 1971.

Below: A zoo employee feeds the penguins at the Milwaukee County Zoo.

German fall festival. German songs and dances are performed, and German foods are served. "Brats" are a popular German food. Brat stands for bratwurst, a German sausage.

Say brat *like* rot *with a* b *in front.*

Southeast Wisconsin has many other attractions. Yerkes Observatory is west of Kenosha on Lake Geneva. The world's largest refracting telescope can be seen there. Its lens is 40 inches across.

A refracting telescope uses a lens as its main way for focusing.

Old World Wisconsin is southwest of Milwaukee near the town of Eagle. It has more than forty old farmhouses and shops. They were built by immigrants in the architectural styles of their homelands. Many of the old buildings were moved there from their original locations across the state. Going to Old World Wisconsin is like stepping back into the past. Guides dressed in clothing of the 1800s explain how the pioneers lived.

Left: Milwaukee's Mitchell Park Conservatory Right: Yerkes Observatory

Aztalan State Park is a short drive northwest from Old World Wisconsin. An ancient Indian town of five hundred people once stood on the site. The early Indians built mounds there about eight hundred years ago.

In nearby Watertown, Margarethe Schurz founded the nation's first kindergarten in 1856. Visitors can go inside the first kindergarten building. Also in Watertown is the fifty-seven-room Octagon House. It was built before the Civil War. The house has five floors that are reached by a circular stairway.

MADISON

Madison, in south-central Wisconsin, is the capital. The town was begun in 1837. Madison has been Wisconsin's capital since 1838. Today, Madison is Wisconsin's second-biggest city.

Madison is one of the prettiest of the fifty state capitals. The city's downtown lies between two lovely lakes—Mendota and Monona. The state capitol rises nearly 300 feet over downtown Madison.

The largest branch of the University of Wisconsin is in Madison. This famous school's sports teams are called the Badgers. The State

University of Wisconsin students gather on the terrace of the Student Union.

The state capitol, in Madison

Historical Society Museum is also in Madison. Fine displays on Wisconsin's Indians can be seen there. The Madison Children's Museum is another highlight of the capital.

SOUTHWEST WISCONSIN

Southwest Wisconsin doesn't have any very large cities. La Crosse is the region's biggest city. La Crosse was founded on the Mississippi River in

1842. It is known for its beautiful scenery. Many people take Mississippi River cruises from La Crosse. One cruise ship is a replica of a paddle-wheel riverboat.

Southwest Wisconsin has great beauty. Thousands of farms can be seen in this hilly region. There are also many charming little towns.

New Glarus is southeast of La Crosse. It is known as "America's Little Switzerland." Swiss people founded the town in 1845. Buildings there show what Swiss pioneer life was like. Visitors can buy Swiss lace and taste Swiss food. Each year the town holds a festival.

Miners from Cornwall, in England, settled nearby Mineral Point during the 1830s. They built houses on a hill above the mines. Old homes of miners can be seen along Mineral Point's Shake Rag Alley. Visitors to Mineral Point can taste Cornish pasties. A pasty is a meat pie. It is made of chopped beef, onions, and potatoes baked in a crust.

Little Norway is northeast of Mineral Point. It is a Norwegian farm from the 1850s. Guides in Norwegian dress take visitors on tours.

The hills of southwest Wisconsin contain many caves. The state's most colorful cave is Cave of the Mounds. It is near Little Norway. Visitors can enter

Below: Viterbo College students in La Crosse

Say pasty *like* past *with an* ee *at the end.*

this fascinating cave. Inside are wonders that took nature over a million years to create.

Baraboo is north of Cave of the Mounds. In 1884, Albert, Otto, Alfred, Charles, and John Ringling began a circus in Baraboo. The Ringling Brothers Circus became very famous. Circus World Museum is in Baraboo. Old circus equipment can be seen there. Live circus shows are performed under a "big top."

The Wisconsin Dells is near Baraboo. There, over the ages, the Wisconsin River carved canyons and cliffs. Many people tour the Dells by boat. There are many strange and beautiful rock formations at the Dells. They include Fat Man's Misery, Devil's Elbow, Witches Gulch, Swallows' Nests, Chimney Rock, and Demon's Anvil.

Two of the main attractions in and near Baraboo are the Circus World Museum (above) and the Wisconsin Dells (left).

43

THE LAKE WINNEBAGO AND GREEN BAY REGIONS

Early airplanes take part in the Oshkosh EAA fly-in.

The team was named the Packers because its founder worked for a meat-packing company. As of 1991, the Packers had won eleven championships —more than any other team in the National Football League.

Lake Winnebago is northeast of the Dells. The town of Ripon is west of the lake. In 1854, local residents met to discuss politics and slavery. This meeting was held at Ripon's "Little White Schoolhouse." It was one of the meetings that led to the founding of the Republican party.

Oshkosh is northeast of Ripon on Lake Winnebago. Each summer, the Experimental Aircraft Association (EAA) holds its fly-in in Oshkosh. Huge crowds come to see old and experimental planes in action.

Appleton is just north of Lake Winnebago. As a child, the great magician Harry Houdini lived in Appleton. Items Houdini used in his magic acts can be seen at Appleton's Outagamie Museum.

The town of Green Bay is northeast of Appleton. The city lies at the southern end of a bay that is also called Green Bay. Green Bay became Wisconsin's first permanent settlement during the 1740s. Today, Green Bay has almost 100,000 people. It is the state's third-largest city.

Green Bay is home to the pro football Packers. The Green Bay Packer Hall of Fame is across from Lambeau Field. That is the team's home field. The

National Railroad Museum is also in Green Bay. The old trains there tell the story of America's railroads. Green Bay also has several paper mills.

The Door Peninsula, or Door County, is northeast of Green Bay. It is the state's "thumb." The passage between the top of the thumb and Washington Island is called *Porte des Morts* ("Death's Door"). The French gave it this name because so many ships were wrecked there. Today, the Door Peninsula is a popular vacation area. People go there to fish, boat, swim, and hike.

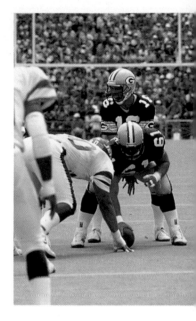

The Green Bay Packers

THE NORTH WOODS

Heading into northern Wisconsin, there is a change in scenery. Towns get fewer and farther between. Trees and lakes become more plentiful. This is Paul Bunyan Country—the North Woods.

The woods are rich with wildlife. More deer than people live there. Black bears roam about looking for berries and nuts. Beavers build their dams on woodland streams. Hikers may spot foxes, porcupines, raccoons, bobcats, and badgers. Coyotes howl at night.

Peshtigo is an interesting town north of Green Bay. Peshtigo was rebuilt after the fire of 1871. The

There were about a million and a half deer in Wisconsin as of 1991.

Rafting is a popular sport on Wisconsin's Wolf River.

Peshtigo Fire Museum has melted coins and other items that survived the fire.

Many northern Wisconsin cities have paper and lumber mills. Marinette, Wausau, and Stevens Point are a few of Wisconsin's mill cities. Trees are turned into paper and lumber in their mills. Today, Wisconsin's woodlands are protected. Rangers guard against fire. Lumber companies plant new trees to replace those they cut down.

Tourism is also important to northern Wisconsin. Cross-country skiing and snowmobiling attract many winter vacationers. Each January, Eagle River hosts the World Championship Snowmobile Derby. Each February, the nation's biggest cross-country ski race is held in Wisconsin. It is called the American Birkebeiner.

Northern Wisconsin is also a fishing paradise. Hayward even has a fishing museum. It is called the National Freshwater Fishing Hall of Fame. The building is five stories tall. It is shaped like a fish!

Most of Wisconsin's American Indians live in the north. The Oneidas have a reservation near Green Bay. The Menominees have a big reservation west of Peshtigo. The Chippewas have several reservations. The Chippewa Museum can be visited at their Lac du Flambeau Reservation.

Lake Superior splashes against northwest Wisconsin. The city of Superior lies on the lake. It is across the lake from Duluth, Minnesota. Superior is a center for repairing ships. It is also a major Lake Superior port. Iron and grain shipped from Superior go to many cities of the world.

A good place to end a Wisconsin trip is the Apostle Islands. They are in Lake Superior. The Apostles can be reached by boat from the town of Bayfield. Every spring, birds stop at the islands before flying across Lake Superior.

The Apostle Islands

The French built a fort on Madeline Island in the Apostles in 1693.

A Gallery
of Famous
Wisconsinites

A Gallery of Famous Wisconsinites

Wisconsin has produced many famous people. They include authors, athletes, actors, and a magician. **John Muir** (1838-1914) was born in Scotland. His family moved to a farm near Portage, Wisconsin, in 1849. Muir became a naturalist. Through his efforts, two national parks were founded in California in 1890. They are Yosemite and Sequoia national parks. Muir also founded the Sierra Club. It works to protect the beauties of nature.

Vinnie Ream Hoxie (1847-1914) was born in Madison. She became a famous sculptor. When she was only eighteen, she made a statue of Abraham Lincoln. Many years later, she helped make a statue of Cherokee scholar Sequoyah. Both statues can be seen in the U.S. Capitol.

Frank Lloyd Wright (1867-1959) was born in Richland Center. He became a great architect. Wright designed the Imperial Hotel in Tokyo, Japan, to withstand earthquakes. This hotel survived a huge earthquake that wrecked much of Tokyo in 1923. Taliesin, Wright's home near Spring Green, was another of his works.

John Muir (above) was a naturalist. Naturalists study plants, animals, and other aspects of nature.

Opposite page (left to right): Carrie, Mary, and Laura Ingalls

49

Two famous Wisconsin natives were magician Harry Houdini (left) and military leader Billy Mitchell (right).

Milwaukee's airport is called Mitchell Field in honor of "Billy" Mitchell.

Ehrich Weiss (1874-1926) grew up in Appleton and Milwaukee. Later, he took the name **Harry Houdini**. He became the most famous magician in American history. He was known for his amazing escapes. He once escaped from a locked box that was dropped into a river.

William L. "Billy" Mitchell (1879-1936) grew up in Milwaukee. Mitchell became a U.S. Army general. In 1918, he led the largest air attack of World War I. Later, he complained that the United States didn't have enough air power. In 1947, the U.S. Air Force was created. This was partly a result of Mitchell's earlier efforts.

Golda Meir (1898-1978) moved to Milwaukee when she was eight years old. She taught school there for a time. In 1921, Meir moved to Palestine (later called Israel). There, she became a lawmaker. Meir served as Israel's first woman prime minister. She headed Israel's government from 1969 to 1974.

America's highest court is the U.S. Supreme Court. Its head judge is the chief justice. In 1986, **William Rehnquist** became chief justice. He was born in Milwaukee in 1924.

Wisconsin has produced many fine authors. Playwright and novelist **Thornton Wilder** (1897-1975) was born in Madison. He won Pulitzer Prizes for three plays, including *Our Town*.

Laura Ingalls Wilder (1867-1957) was born in Pepin. She wrote novels for young people about pioneer life. *Little House on the Prairie* is one of her best-known works.

Marguerite Henry was another children's writer. She was born in Milwaukee in 1902. At the age of eleven, she sold a story to a magazine. Later, she wrote novels about horses. She received the 1949 Newbery Medal for *King of the Wind*.

Several great actors were also born in Wisconsin. Theater actor **Alfred Lunt** (1893-1977)

Political leader Golda Meir

Children's writer Marguerite Henry

Actor Spencer Tracy

Actor Gene Wilder (left) and actor-director Orson Welles (right)

and his wife, Lynn Fontanne, were the most famous couple on the American stage.

Film star **Fredric March** (1897-1975) was born in Racine. He won two Academy Awards. Film star **Spencer Tracy** (1900-1967) was a Milwaukee native. Tracy won Academy Awards for roles in *Captains Courageous* and in *Boys Town.* **Gene Wilder** (born in 1935) is another Milwaukee native. Wilder starred in *Willy Wonka and the Chocolate Factory* and in *Young Frankenstein.*

Actor-director **Orson Welles** (1915-1985) was born in Kenosha. In 1938, he directed the famous radio broadcast called *War of the Worlds.* It was about invaders from Mars. Many listeners thought Martians had really landed! In 1941, Welles acted in and directed *Citizen Kane.* Many people call it the greatest film ever made.

Wisconsin is also well known for its sports figures. Football star **Elroy "Crazy Legs" Hirsch** was one of Wisconsin's great athletes. Hirsch was born in Wausau in 1923. He starred for the University of Wisconsin and the Los Angeles Rams. He was elected to the Football Hall of Fame in 1968. Then, he served as the University of Wisconsin's athletic director (1969-1986).

Baseball star **Harvey Kuenn** (1930-1988) was born in West Allis. Kuenn won the 1959 American League batting crown. In 1982, Kuenn managed the Milwaukee Brewers to the American League pennant.

Speed skater **Eric Heiden** was born in Madison in 1958. Heiden won all five men's speed-skating races at the 1980 Winter Olympics. He set a new Olympic record in all five races.

The birthplace of Laura Ingalls Wilder, Orson Welles, "Fighting Bob" La Follette, Eric Heiden, and Frank Lloyd Wright . . .

The place where malted milk, the typewriter, and America's first kindergarten had their starts . . .

The state that is first in producing milk, butter, cheese, and paper . . .

This is Wisconsin—the Badger State!

Elroy "Crazy Legs" Hirsch

Did You Know?

Facial tissue was invented in Neenah, Wisconsin, in the early 1900s.

In 1878, Wisconsin's state government held the world's first auto race. It offered $10,000 to the person whose auto could go the fastest from Green Bay to Madison. Two autos, one from Green Bay and the other from Oshkosh, were the only two entrants. The Oshkosh car won the 200-mile race with an average speed of 6 miles per hour.

Henry "Hank" Aaron holds the career record for big-league homers with 755. Aaron spent most of his career in Milwaukee. He played for the Milwaukee Braves (1954-1965) and the Atlanta Braves (1966-1974), and later for the Milwaukee Brewers (1975-1976).

Wisconsin has towns named Luck, Ladysmith, Pound, Friendship, Tigerton, and Footville.

As a young man, John Muir invented an "early-rising machine." This strange alarm clock was hooked up to a leg of his bed. When the clock went off, the leg was loosened and Muir was awakened by being dumped to the floor.

October 31 is Halloween. Because Harry Houdini died on Halloween in 1926, magicians celebrate the week that includes October 31 as National Magic Week.

An old Wisconsin saying is: The world is your cow, but you'll have to do the milking.

The largest white poplar tree on earth is at Fond du Lac. It is 96 feet tall. Its trunk measures 21 feet around.

Wisconsin's Walter Goodland was the oldest state governor in United States history. Goodland governed Wisconsin from 1943 to 1947. He died in office at the age of eighty-four.

Wisconsin has more than a dozen official symbols—one of the largest totals among the fifty states. It all began in 1893 when schoolchildren voted the sugar maple the state tree.

A hunting dog called the American water spaniel was developed in the Midwest around 1880. It became Wisconsin's state dog in 1986.

Wisconsin also has towns named Bear Creek, Beaver Dam, Buffalo, Eagle, Elk Mound, and Pigeon Falls.

The high school sports teams in Monroe, Wisconsin, are called the Monroe Cheesemakers.

Author Maureen Daly grew up in Fond du Lac. She was only twenty-one years old when *Seventeenth Summer,* her famous novel for teenagers, was published.

WISCONSIN INFORMATION

The state flag

American water spaniels

Badger

Area: 56,153 square miles (twenty-sixth biggest of the fifty states)

Greatest Distance North to South: 315 miles

Greatest Distance East to West: 295 miles

Borders: Lake Superior and Upper Michigan to the north; Lake Michigan to the east; Illinois to the south; Iowa and Minnesota to the west

Highest Point: Timms Hill, 1,952 feet above sea level

Lowest Point: Along Lake Michigan's shore, 581 feet above sea level

Hottest Recorded Temperature: 114° F. (at the Wisconsin Dells, on July 13, 1936)

Coldest Recorded Temperature: -54° F. (at Danbury, on January 24, 1922)

Statehood: The thirtieth state, on May 29, 1848

Origin of Name: *Wisconsin* comes from the Chippewa word *Weeskonsan.* It was the Chippewa name for the Wisconsin River and may mean "the gathering of waters."

Capital: Madison

Previous Capitals: Belmont (1836) and Burlington (1837-1838), which is now in Iowa

Counties: 72

United States Representatives: 9 (as of 1992)

State Senators: 33

State Representatives: 99

State Song: "On, Wisconsin!" (words by J. S. Hubbard and Charles D. Rosa; melody by William T. Purdy)

State Motto: "Forward"

Nicknames: "Badger State," "America's Dairyland," "Land of Lakes"

State Seal: Adopted in 1881

State Flag: Adopted in its present form in 1981

State Flower: Wood violet

State Bird: Robin

State Tree: Sugar maple

State Animal: Badger

State Fish: Muskellunge, known for short as the "muskie"

State Dog: American water spaniel

State Farm Animal: Dairy cow

State Fossil: Trilobite

State Mineral: Galena

State Rock: Red granite

State Drink: Milk

State Insect: Honeybee

State Wildlife Animal: White-tailed deer

Wood violets

Some Rivers: Mississippi, St. Croix, Wisconsin, Chippewa, Rock, Wolf, Fox, Brule, Flambeau

Wildlife: Deer, black bears, beavers, foxes, porcupines, raccoons, badgers, skunks, coyotes, bobcats, wolves, eagles, Canada geese, ducks, partridges, loons, robins, many other kinds of birds, muskellunge (muskies), trout, bass, sturgeon, whitefish, salmon, many other kinds of fish

Farm Products: Milk, beef cattle, hogs, sweet corn, snap beans, peas, beets, cranberries, oats, carrots, cucumbers for pickles, hay, maple syrup

Mining Products: Crushed stone, sand and gravel

Manufactured Products: Farm machinery and other machinery, paper, packaged milk, butter, cheese, ice cream, beer, meat, auto engines and other auto parts, furniture, tools and many other kinds of metal goods, plumbing fixtures, scientific equipment

Population: 4,891,769, sixteenth among the fifty states (1990 U.S. Census Bureau figures)

Major Cities (1990 state census figures):

Maple tree

Dairy cattle

Milwaukee	628,088	Appleton	65,695
Madison	191,262	West Allis	63,221
Green Bay	96,466	Waukesha	56,958
Racine	84,298	Eau Claire	56,856
Kenosha	80,352	Oshkosh	55,006

Wisconsin History

10,000 B.C.—Prehistoric peoples reach Wisconsin

1634—French explorer Jean Nicolet reaches Wisconsin

1654-59—Fur traders Pierre Esprit, Sieur de Radisson, and Medard Chouart, Sieur des Groseilliers, explore Wisconsin

1671-1763—The French rule Wisconsin

1684—The French build a trading post at Green Bay

1718—The French build a fort at Green Bay

1745—Green Bay becomes Wisconsin's first permanent settlement

1763—The English take control of Wisconsin

1783—Wisconsin becomes part of the United States

1787—Wisconsin becomes part of the Northwest Territory

1800—Wisconsin becomes part of the Indiana Territory

1809—Wisconsin becomes part of the Illinois Territory

1818—Wisconsin becomes part of the Michigan Territory

1832—The Sauk and Fox are crushed in the Battle of Bad Axe in southwest Wisconsin, ending the Black Hawk War

1833—Solomon Juneau founds a settlement that becomes Milwaukee

1836—The U.S. government creates the Wisconsin Territory

1848—Wisconsin becomes the thirtieth state on May 29

1850—The population of Wisconsin is 305,391

1854—A founding meeting of the Republican party is held at Ripon

1856—Margarethe Schurz opens America's first kindergarten at Watertown

1862-65—During the Civil War, about 90,000 Wisconsinites fight for the Union

1871—About 1,200 people die in the Peshtigo Fire

Costumed guides at Old World Wisconsin demonstrate the daily activities of the early settlers.

1890—Dr. Stephen Babcock develops the Babcock Test to measure the butterfat content of milk

1900—The population of Wisconsin is 2,069,042

1901—"Fighting Bob" La Follette becomes governor and begins making improvements in the state

1917-18—About 120,000 Wisconsin men and women serve during World War I

1929-39—The Great Depression hits America; many factories and farms go out of business in Wisconsin

1932—Wisconsin passes the first state law to provide money for jobless people

1941-45—After the United States enters World War II, about 300,000 Wisconsin men and women help win the war

1948—Happy one-hundredth birthday, Badger State!

1950—Wisconsin's population is 3,434,575

1957—The Milwaukee Braves win the World Series

1967—The Green Bay Packers win the first Super Bowl

1968—The Green Bay Packers win the Super Bowl again

1969—Golda Meir, who grew up and taught school in Milwaukee, becomes prime minister of Israel

1971—The Milwaukee Bucks win the pro basketball championship

1982—A big project to rebuild and beautify downtown Milwaukee is completed; the Milwaukee Brewers win the World Series

1986—Milwaukee-born William Rehnquist becomes chief justice of the U.S. Supreme Court

1987—Tommy Thompson becomes governor

1990—The population of the Badger State reaches 4,891,769

Robert M. La Follette

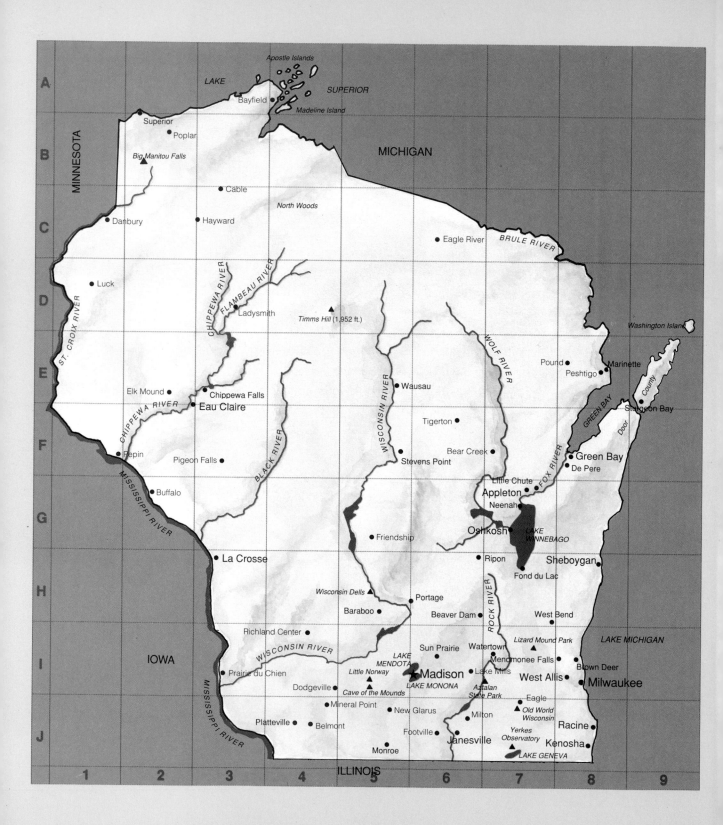

A LAKE SUPERIOR
Apostle Islands
Bayfield
Madeline Island
MICHIGAN

MINNESOTA

Superior
Poplar
B Big Manitou Falls

Cable
North Woods

Danbury Hayward
C Eagle River BRULE RIVER

Luck

ST. CROIX RIVER
D Ladysmith Timms Hill (1,952 ft.) WOLF RIVER Washington Island

CHIPPEWA RIVER
FLAMBEAU RIVER

Pound
Marinette
E Elk Mound Wausau Peshtigo Sturgeon Bay
Chippewa Falls WISCONSIN RIVER Door County
Eau Claire CHIPPEWA RIVER Tigerton GREEN BAY

Bear Creek
Pigeon Falls BLACK RIVER Green Bay
F Pepin Stevens Point Little Chute De Pere
MISSISSIPPI RIVER Appleton FOX RIVER
Buffalo Neenah

G Friendship Oshkosh LAKE WINNEBAGO
La Crosse Ripon Sheboygan
Fond du Lac

H Wisconsin Dells Portage ROCK RIVER West Bend LAKE MICHIGAN
Baraboo Beaver Dam

Richland Center Lizard Mound Park
I WISCONSIN RIVER Sun Prairie Watertown Menomonee Falls Brown Deer
IOWA Prairie du Chien LAKE MENDOTA Madison West Allis Milwaukee
Little Norway Lake Mills
Dodgeville LAKE MONONA Aztalan State Park
Cave of the Mounds Eagle
Mineral Point New Glarus Old World Racine
J Platteville Belmont Milton Wisconsin
Footville Yerkes Kenosha
Monroe Janesville Observatory
LAKE GENEVA

ILLINOIS

1   2   3   4   5   6   7   8   9

MAP KEY

Apostle Islands	A4	Milton	J6
Appleton	G7	Milwaukee	I8
Aztalan State Park	I6,7	Mineral Point	J4
Baraboo	H5	Mississippi River	
Bayfield	A3		F,G,H,I,J1,2,3
Bear Creek	F7	Monroe	J5
Beaver Dam	H6	Neenah	G7
Belmont	J4	New Glarus	J5
Big Manitou Falls	B2	North Woods	C4
Black River	F,G3,4	Old World Wisconsin	J7
Brown Deer	I8	Oshkosh	G7
Brule River	C7	Pepin	F1,2
Buffalo	G2	Peshtigo	E8
Cable	C3	Pigeon Falls	F3
Cave of the Mounds	I5	Platteville	J4
Chippewa Falls	E3	Poplar	B3
Chippewa River	D,E,F2,3	Portage	H6
Danbury	C1	Pound	E8
De Pere	F8	Prairie du Chien	I3
Dodgeville	I4	Racine	J8
Door County	E,F8,9	Richland Center	I4
Eagle	I7	Ripon	H,I6
Eagle River	C6	Rock River	H7
Eau Claire	F3	St. Croix River	D,E1
Elk Mound	E2	Sheboygan	H8
Flambeau River	D3	Stevens Point	F5
Fond du Lac	H7	Sturgeon Bay	E,F9
Footville	J6	Sun Prairie	I6
Fox River	F,G7,8	Superior	B2
Friendship	G5	Tigerton	F6
Green Bay (bay)	E,F8	Timms Hill	D4
Green Bay (city)	F8	Washington Island	D9
Hayward	C3	Watertown	I7
Janesville	J6	Wausau	E5
Kenosha	J8	West Allis	I8
La Crosse	H3	West Bend	H7
Ladysmith	D3	Wisconsin Dells	H5
Lake Geneva	J7	Wisconsin River	
Lake Mendota	I5		E,F,G,H,I4,5
Lake Michigan		Wolf River	E7
	F,G,H,I,J8,9	Yerkes Observatory	J7
Lake Mills	I6		
Lake Monona	I6		
Lake Superior	A3,4		
Lake Winnebago	G7		
Little Chute	G7		
Little Norway	I5		
Lizard Mound Park	I7		
Luck	D1		
Madeline Island	A4		
Madison	I6		
Marinette	E8		
Menomonee Falls	I7,8		

GLOSSARY

allies: Nations that help one another, especially during a war

ancestor: A person from whom one is descended, such as a grandfather or a great-grandmother

ancient: Relating to those living at a time early in history

antislavery: Against slavery

billion: A thousand million (1,000,000,000)

brewery: A place where beer is made

canoe: A narrow boat covered with birchbark that was invented by the Indians

capital: The city that is the seat of government

capitol: The building in which the government meets

climate: The typical weather of a region

dairies: Businesses that are concerned with producing milk products such as butter and cheese

explorers: People who visit and study unknown lands

glaciers: Masses of slowly moving ice

independence: Freedom from being controlled by another

lumberjacks: People who cut down trees for lumber companies

manufacturing: The making of products

million: A thousand thousand (1,000,000)

mission: A little settlement based around a church

permanent: Lasting

pollute: To make dirty

population: The number of people in a place

poverty: A lack of money

sculptor: An artist who carves, chisels, or molds hard materials

slavery: A practice in which some people are owned by other people

territory: Land owned by a country

tourism: The business of providing services such as food and lodging for travelers

PICTURE ACKNOWLEDGMENTS

Front cover, © H. Abernathy/**H. Armstrong Roberts**; 1, © **Tom Dietrich**; 2, **Tom Dunnington**; 3, © Robert Frerck/**Odyssey Productions**; 5, **Tom Dunnington**; 6-7, © Tom Algire Photography/**Tom Stack & Associates**; 8, © **Tom Till/Photographer**; 9 (left), © Tom Algire Photography/**Tom Stack & Associates**; 9 (right), **Courtesy of Hammond, Incorporated, Maplewood, New Jersey**; 10 (both pictures), © **Tom Till/Photographer**; 11 (left), © **Jerry Hennen**; 11 (right), © **Tom Till/Photographer**; 12-13, © **James P. Rowan**; 15, © Richard L. Capps/**R/C Photo Agency**; 16 (left), © James P. Rowan/**Tony Stone Worldwide/Chicago Ltd.**; 16 (right), © **Joan Dunlop**; 17, © **James P. Rowan**; 18, © **H. Armstrong Roberts**; 19, **Hand Colored by North Wind Picture Archives**; 20, **Hand Colored by North Wind Picture Archives**; 21, © Skip Drew; 22 (left), **Hand Colored by North Wind Picture Archives**; 22 (right), **Historical Pictures Service, Chicago**; 24, **Historical Pictures Service, Chicago**; 25, **AP/Wide World Photos**; 26, **UPI/Bettmann**; 27, **AP/Wide World Photos**; 28, © Robert Frerck/**Odyssey Productions**; 29 (left), © **Joseph A. DiChello, Jr.**; 29 (right), © **Joan Dunlop**; 30, © Robert Frerck/**Odyssey Productions**; 31 (left), © Doris De Witt/**Tony Stone Worldwide/Chicago Ltd.**; 31 (right), © **Cameramann International, Ltd.**; 32, © Richard L. Capps/**R/C Photo Agency**; 33 (left), © Paul Damien/**Tony Stone Worldwide/Chicago Ltd.**; 33 (right), © **Cameramann International Ltd.**; 34-35, © F. Sieb/**H. Armstrong Roberts**; 36, **Historical Pictures Service, Chicago**; 37, © Scott Berner/**Marilyn Gartman Agency**; 38, © **Joseph A. DiChello, Jr.**; 39 (left), © J. Blank/**H. Armstrong Roberts**; 39 (right), © **James P. Rowan**; 40, © Roger A. Lloyd/**H. Armstrong Roberts**; 41, © Scott Berner/**Marilyn Gartman Agency**; 42, © **Larsh K. Bristol Photo**; 43 (bottom), © Tom Algire/**Tom Stack & Associates**; 43 (right), © **Joan Dunlop**; 44, © **Jerry Hennen**; 45, **Wisconsin Tourism Development**; 46, © **James P. Rowan**; 47, © Tom Stack/**Tom Stack & Associates**; 48, **Laura Ingalls Wilder Memorial Society, De Smet, South Dakota**; 49, **North Wind Picture Archives**; 50 (left), © 1980, Robert Lee Jacobs, used by permission of the publisher, Lee Jacobs Production, Pomeroy, Ohio 45769; 50 (right), **Historical Pictures Service, Chicago**; 51 (both pictures), **AP/Wide World Photos**; 52 (top), **Historical Pictures Service, Chicago**; 52 (bottom), **AP/Wide World Photos**; 53, **AP/Wide World Photos**; 54 (left), **Courtesy of the Kimberly-Clark Corporation**; 54 (right), **AP/Wide World Photos**; 55, © **James P. Rowan**; 56 (top), **Courtesy of Flag Research Center, Winchester, Massachusetts 01890**; 56 (middle), **American Kennel Club**; 56 (bottom), © E. Degginger/**H. Armstrong Roberts**; 57 (top and middle), © **Jerry Hennen**; 57 (bottom), © Robert Frerck/**Tony Stone Worldwide/Chicago Ltd.**; 58, © Richard L. Capps/**R/C Photo Agency**; 59, **Historical Pictures Service, Chicago**; 60, **Tom Dunnington**; back cover, © Terry Donnell/**Tom Stack & Associates**

INDEX

Page numbers in boldface type indicate illustrations.

ABOUT THE AUTHOR

Dennis Brindell Fradin is the author of 150 published children's books. His works for Childrens Press include the Young People's Stories of Our States series, the Disaster! series, and the Thirteen Colonies series. Dennis is married to Judith Bloom Fradin, who taught high-school and college English for many years. She is now Dennis's chief researcher. The Fradins are the parents of two sons, Anthony and Michael, and a daughter, Diana. Dennis graduated from Northwestern University in 1967 with a B.A. in creative writing, and has lived in Evanston, Illinois, since that year.